From the Law of Nations to the Emergence of International Law

Jean-Paul Coujou

Foreword by Robert Fastiggi

En Route Books and Media, LLC
Saint Louis, MO

⊛ *ENROUTE*
Make the time

En Route Books and Media, LLC
5705 Rhodes Avenue
St. Louis, MO 63109

Contact us at
contactus@enroutebooksandmedia.com

Cover Credit: Sebastian Mahfood
Copyright 2025 Jean-Paul Coujou

ISBN-13: 979-8-88870-324-3
Library of Congress Control Number: 9798888703243

All rights reserved. No part of this book may be reproduced, stored in a retrieval system, or transmitted in any form, or by any means, electronic, mechanical, photocopying, or otherwise, without the prior written permission of the author.

Table of Contents

Presentation iii

Foreword v

Introduction 1

I: Origin and Development of the Concept 3

II: The Emergence of a Legal Understanding of the Law of Nations 13

III: From the Law of Nations to the Emergence of International Law 21

IV: Necessity of the Distinction between the Law of Nations and Natural Law in Sixteenth-Century Second Scholasticism 47

V: Historical Justification of the Law of Nations ... 59

Conclusion 69

Bibliography 71

About the Author 79

Presentation

An analysis of the origins and changes in the law of nations from Antiquity to the emergence of modernity reveals how this same law contributes—through the legal development of humanity that it makes possible—to understanding humanity as the architect of its own improvement. After a long process, the reconciliation of natural law and the law of nations found its first expression in the Universal Declaration of Human Rights.

This book was previously published in French as *Aux origines du droit international. Le droit des gens* (Paris: Uppreditions, Paris, 2016). The English translation is by the author.

Foreword

Many Catholics are familiar with the distinctions between the revealed divine law, the natural law, and the civil law, but not many are familiar with the *ius gentium,* or the law of nations. In this carefully researched and clearly-written book, Jean-Paul Coujou traces the origins of the law of nations from its Greco-Roman roots, its subsequent Patristic and medieval developments, and finally into its more complete elaboration during the second scholastic period with thinkers such as Francisco de Vitoria, O.P (c.1483-1546) and Francisco Suárez, S.J. (1548-1617). A greater appreciation of the human race as a universal community of peoples (*communitas totus orbis*) emerged during this period.

Although the human race is divided into multiple peoples and states, there is a fundamental unity grounded in a common rational nature and the natural law. The unity of the human race forms a basis for the development of international law. According to Suárez, man, by his rational nature, has a political end that can only be realized in the heart of a peaceful order in which the different states cooperate with each other. Suárez also believes the unity of the human race should be governed by "the precept of mutual love and mercy, a precept that extends to all, even to strangers, and of any condition whatsoever" (*De legibus* lib. 2, cap. 19, n. 9). This mutual love provides a basis for human rights and mutual assistance. Because no nation will ever be completely self-sufficient, Suárez affirms the need for some type of international law that can direct and order exchanges among nations.

The law of nations is related to the natural law, but it is distinct from it. The law of nations belongs to the sphere of positive law, since this law only becomes effective by being enforced by a human will that makes the universal values of the natural law suitable to historical variations.

Because of the historical constitution of the human community, various human laws emerge. These human laws can be civil laws that are written and specific. There are, though, unwritten human laws that are grounded in custom. The precepts of the law of nations must be distinguished from the precepts of the civil law because they are not constituted by written laws but by customs, which are not specific to any single country but to the totality or quasi-totality of nations. The law of nations is further developed by later natural law thinkers such as Grotius (1583-1645), Samuel Pufendorf (1632-1694), Jean Barbeyrac (1674-1744), and Jean-Jacques Burlamaqui (1694-1748). These thinkers believe the law of nations can serve as a basis for common agreement among peoples and states, which constitutes the essence of international law.

Professor Coujou is one of the world's leading experts on the metaphysics and political thought of early modern scholasticism. This present work is a testimony to his erudition and clarity of thought. *From the law of nations to international law* provides a much-needed historical overview of how international law emerged from the concept of the *ius gentium*, the law of nations.

Robert Fastiggi, Ph.D.
Professor of Dogmatic Theology,
Sacred Heart Major Seminary,
Detroit, Michigan

Introduction

In order to be formulated as such, the question of the law of nations (*ius gentium*)—or the law of peoples—requires reference to the key concepts that preceded it and were formulated by Greek thought. Thus the opposition between natural law and positive law, or between an existing effective law and an ideal law, is at the origin of the concept of the law of nations.

On the one hand, positive law only exists on the basis of an effective social and political force; it is established by custom or by a legislative power and, consequently, instituted by men. It is essentially historical, and the condition for its emergence and preservation is a determined social force. In this sense, it is similar to a right resulting from the dedication of power relations that preceded it. On the other hand, natural law, as a system of norms of justice, prescribes, on the basis of these norms, a specific form of behavior, either of men individually, or of their relations as individuals to the community of men. As a normative law embodying values presented as necessary and universal, it is identifiable as an invariable law, independent of historical evolution and expressing the non-historicity of nature.

This right is not the result of a human creation; on the contrary, it is up to mankind to discover it on the basis of knowledge of the universal order and the study of human nature. Its status as an ideal derives from the fact that it is made up of values that cannot be fulfilled by existing law. It is on the basis of this distinction that the specific nature of the concept of the law of nations will be developed. Thus, a critical historical examination of the law of nations cannot fail to raise three difficulties: 1°) that of its origin, which raises the problem of the relationship between nature and convention, between the universality of natural law and the historical particularity of positive law; 2°) that of its foundation, which requires us to establish the degree to which it is similar to and different from natural law; and 3°) that of its purpose, which creates a path towards the constitution of an ethical and legal future for humanity that respects its diversity.

I

Origin and Development of the Concept

The first traces of the concept of natural law can be found in the thought of Pythagoras (c.570–490 BC), who understood it as the law governing all living beings, whether humans or animals, in consideration of their respective capacity to be significantly affected. This conception was maintained by Roman jurists, notably in the theories of Ulpian (c. 170–228), who took as examples of natural law the relationship between the sexes, procreation and the education of children. A distinction must therefore be drawn between the natural law common to man and animals, the law of nations, which is essentially human, and the civil law specific to the city.

A second conception of natural law was also developed by Sophocles. In his play *Antigone* (c. 450 BC), the main character, Antigone, comments on the laws that transcend the merely human:

> For it was not Zeus who proclaimed it. Nor did Justice, who sits with the gods below, es-

tablish such laws among men. And I did not believe that your edicts were so powerful to give license to a mere mortal to trample on the laws that the gods have placed beyond any code or reach. They do not exist today or yesterday, but from all eternity, and no one knows where they originated. I was not going to allow myself to be intimidated by any human pretense, so that they would condemn me in the court of the gods!

This view of natural law was also developed by Aristotle (384-322 BC), the Stoic school and, in Rome, by Cicero (c. 106–43 BC) and Seneca (c. 1 BC–65 AD). In this sense, the unwritten laws to which Antigone refers—when confronted by Creon in Sophocles' tragedy of the same name—express rules that are recognized by mankind without being set down in a text; they express the aspiration towards a good and a just order that completes and exceeds the rules established by the legislator. And if we consider human laws, they can be likened either to an imperfect duplicate of divine law, or to its imitation, or to its emanation. Antigone synthesizes a conflict of duties between the State, guarantor of compliance with the positivity of the law, and the imperatives of the ethical-religious conscience. It is clear that in examining such a conflict, unwritten laws have a more universal value and are known to all. Their function (in this case, the burial of the dead) is to oppose the contingency and relativity of human laws with intangible principles. These are based on their divine origin and not on human nature as such.

To opt for unwritten laws, as Antigone does, is to show a preference for the divine over the human, for the eternal over that which is subject to corruption. Their religious origin is inseparable from reference to a set of moral values (honor, piety, justice, fidelity, etc.) which ultimately have no more legitimate guarantors than the conscientious judgment of individuals. Paradoxically, unwritten laws are inscribed by the gods in the human conscience in a similar way to the sense of beauty, justice or love for ones nearest and dearest. Nevertheless, although they were initially intended to compensate for the imperfections of written laws, they have undergone an evolution that refocuses them on the human being, at the risk of conferring on the unwritten law, just as it had previously conferred on the written law, an equivalent degree of relativity. Gradually stripping the unwritten law of its divine guarantee threatens to reduce it to a tacit consensus whose claim to universality could then be called into question.

Once unwritten laws can no longer be equated purely and simply with divine laws, they tend to become laws common to a group. The consequence of this is the loss of normative universality in favor of the practical function accorded to a usage. This does not mean, however, that the search for common laws (particularly in relation to the rules of war) is abolished. Such laws are based on general principles that belong to the moral sphere (hospitality, respect for oaths, worship of the dead, etc.) and, by virtue of the defense of civilization that they imply, they characterize the primitive form of the law of nations in Greek culture. Their recognition is made possible by apparently universal consent. As for unwritten laws, they gradually tended to overlap with what came to be known as natural laws.

From the Stoic perspective, of which Cicero (106-43 BC) is one of the leading exponents, this heritage was modified. Natural law becomes specific to man by the very fact that it is founded on the right reason (*recta ratio*) that the divinity has distributed throughout humanity. It embodies a transhistorical, just, and good law which, independently of any human convention, commands man to do good and forbids him to commit evil. The scope of such a right is therefore universal and governs the conduct of all peoples. No one can be exempt from its commandments, and no human law can derogate from them, no more than the authority of an institution or the invocation of social interests. The result is the thesis, defended in particular by Roman jurists such as Gaius (130–180 AD), that natural law, which is consubstantial with the human race, is ontologically and ethically prior to conventional law. From then on, a bipartite classification must be taken into account between 1°) the law of nations, identifiable as a set of rules respected by peoples and established by the natural order of things, which tends to make it natural law; and 2°) the civil law specific to each city.

Greek thought, particularly with Aristotle, invoked a common and universal law that was appropriate to nature. Aristotle drew a distinction between the absolute right, which expresses the moral virtue of justice as a disposition to preserve or restore equality in relations with others, and the political right, which is inseparable from the sphere of legislation. In particular, this led to a distinction being drawn in political law between natural law, which is universally valid regardless of time or place, and positive or legal law based on convention. With natural law, Aristotle asserts a norm that is irreducible to the positivity of laws. However, if the law is based on principles of natural law, its effectiveness depends on an assessment of the conditions of its application, which have to do with fairness; indeed, it is inconceivable for the Greek man to claim to impose on the nature of things abstract universal principles from which reality should be deduced.

The Romans reshaped this heritage by integrating it into their constitution of a legal science based on the rigorous formulation of the divisions of the subjects of law. This science includes an enumeration of the precepts of law—thus the duty to live in accordance with what is honest—the law being understood as the art of goodness and equality. From this point on, it is proper principally to mention, the division of law into: 1°) civil law, the law of nations, and natural law, 2°) written law and unwritten law, and 3°) public law and private law. As Gaius explains in the *Institutes* (I, 2, 1): "What natural reason establishes in all men, what all nations observe, is called the law of nations;" the very existence of written law and its predecessor, custom, historically implies that a people must comply with rules that are specific to it, but also with rules that are common to the whole of the human race. It follows that there is a distinction between the civil law that a nation has attributed to itself, specific to a city, and the law of nations to which all peoples conform in a similar way; the latter originates in what natural reason establishes for humanity, thereby expressing a right that all men use because they belong to the same species.

Civil law (*jus civile*) can be identified with a right that is specific to each State and concerns only its citizens; in Rome, it corresponds to the right that can legitimately be claimed by its citizens. The law of nations very precisely represents the law exercised in the Roman state over both citizens and foreigners. It also refers, in a more extensive and less defined way, to the law that has a common denominator among all peoples and is therefore common to the whole of humanity. As far as natural law is concerned, it is either identified with a law, an ideal standard of positive law, which is close to a law common to all human beings that can actually be referred to as the law of nations; or it corresponds to a law common to all living beings in a way similar to how the law of nations applies to all human beings and the civil law to all citizens. Ultimately, the original distinction between civil law and the law of nations refers to a primary distinction between the rules applying to citizens alone and the rules subsequently established to regulate relations between these same citizens and foreigners admitted to be under the protection of Roman laws.

In this sense, Ulpian's doctrine establishes a clear distinction between natural law and the law of nations. It is based on the opposition between natural law, which is valid for all living beings, and the

Ch. 1: Origin and Development of the Concept

law of nations, which is valid only for the human race and is common to a multitude of peoples. There can be no constant concordance between the two, and slavery—historically introduced by the law of nations—is contrary to the universal values advocated by natural law, namely equality and freedom.

Nevertheless, if we refer to the conception defended by Cicero and Gaius, we find an identification of natural law with the law of nations. The *Digest* (I, 1, 9) defines the law of nations as "the law which natural reason has established between all men and which is equally defended by all peoples." As a result, in addition to slavery, the *Institutes* mention the following as institutions and establishments of the law of nations: wars, captivity, immunity of ambassadors, private property, the construction of dwellings and the division of humanity into multiple nations.

II

The Emergence of a Legal Understanding of the Law of Nations

Christianity, with the Fathers of the Church—St Augustine, Origen and Tertullian– took over and reshaped the dual heritage of Aristotelianism and Roman juridical theory. Thus, in the words of the Apostle Paul in the *Epistle to the Romans*, even if the Law of Moses was not given to the Gentiles, there is, immanent in them, a law written in their hearts. There is, therefore, a natural law engraved by God in the hearts of men, expressing the eternal divine will governing all nations and which, because it was born with man, is not ignored by any of them. The foundation of the legitimacy of laws has no other origin than such eternity.

Isidore of Seville (560-570?- 636) synthesized the teachings of the philosophers, the Church Fathers and the classical jurists into a single body of doctrine. He took up the tripartite division inherited from Roman law, particularly from Ulpian, and assimilated the law of nations to the institutions in use in almost all nations, regardless of whether or not they conformed to natural law. It is precisely positive law established by men. It concerns, for example, wars, captivity, alliances, peace treaties, the inviolability of ambassadors, etc. As far as natural law is concerned, there is no possible similarity with animals; it is fundamentally human and expresses in its own way a normative ideal that can be transposed to all peoples. In terms of the legacy of Roman law, it relates to social categories such as marriage and child-rearing, but it also outlines, in terms of history, an original situation in which men could claim universal freedom and equality. In this sense, Isidore invokes the equal freedom of all and the common possession of all things, which are precisely the basis of natural law, which is to say that this right consists in part in their institutionalization. And the law of nations, for its part, specifically incorporates the conventions and customs in use in almost all nations. Thus, the law created by men, or the law of nations, is characterized by the introduction of the division of property and, by the same token, from a moral perspective, by the advent of greed, which is at the root of wars. As a result, the law of nations conventionally allowed the emergence of private property, slavery and political power, derogating from the principles of natural law and putting an end to the equal freedom of all and the original common possession. The subsequent introduction of civil law, initially understood as a customary law specific to each political community, could then represent the ultimate form of law at the starting point of society as we know it.

These remarks allow us to infer that there are derogations from natural law in the circumstances invoked. Indeed, the freedom of all and common possession refer to a historically obsolete state that resurfaces if it is not acknowledged that it has been expressly subject to derogation. However, no particular authority affirms derogation from natural law; derogation, as confirmed by the law of nations, is a social fact. This does not, however, obscure the function of the establishment of property, which, for Isidore, responds to a use that does not cause harm (*usus innoxius*) and ultimately ensures (by recognizing the other side of the moral thesis that invokes the link between property, greed and war) a coexistence that also aims at pacification through the delimitation of yours and mine.

And if we also consider humanity's historical transition to a plurality of nations, this very differentiation is constitutive of natural law; it is expressed in the right of communication or circulation (*ius communicationis*), an inalienable right (except for reasons of force majeure), and the denial of which gives rise to a *casus belli*. To this right should be added the *ius necessitatis*, the right to respond to a pressing need, implying in situations of extreme necessity the possibility of seizing what is necessary to ensure one's survival; once the urgent need has been met, there is no obligation to return what has been consumed. A principle emerges from this: everyone has the right to do what is urgently beneficial to them, without harming anyone else, in respect of the property of others. In accordance with natural law, it is legitimate to make use of someone else's property if it does no harm to the owner. For Isidore, such use that does not cause harm to others is akin to a natural right in the sense that it constitutes its sphere of exercise.

In Isidore's view, these distinctions should make it possible to differentiate between the order of the lawful or legitimate (*fas*)—to which natural law refers—and the right (*jus*) for which such a determination is not constitutive of its reality. We are therefore faced with the difficulty of determining to what extent 1°) natural law composes the general structure of what is lawful in relation to freedoms and what is permitted, and 2°) to what extent positive law mainly comprises what relates to prohibitions and restrictions. Now, if natural law is to be understood essentially in terms of individual freedom, the difficulty will lie in explaining the relationship between, on the one hand, the order of legitimacy and freedom and, on the other hand, the order of law, which also implies a limitation of natural freedom. With the law of nations, the problem also arises of knowing what limits are placed on the law in its derogation from the imperatives of the sphere of the lawful, which precedes it in the order of existence.

It was only after a long theological, legal and philosophical gestation period—led in particular by Saint Bonaventure (c.1221–1274) and Alexander of Hales (c. 1170–1245)—that the law of nations was considered to be a properly human natural law. It is like a humanly limited historical response to the theological observation of the fallen state of primitive natural law.

Historically, however, as Suarez (1548-1617) pointed out, the first to assign a specific value to the law of nations was Thomas Aquinas (1225-1274). In expounding a theory of the law of nations as customary law, Aquinas drew on the legacy of Aristotelian distinctions between primary and secondary natural law. On the one hand, the law of nations comes under natural law because its precepts are the necessary consequences of the fundamental principles of law and are given to man by natural reason with a view to public utility and tranquility. On the other hand, there is diversity in natural law, which leads to the recognition of a necessary difference with the natural law common to all living beings; this corresponds to primary natural law. However, secondary natural law is only common to human beings; it is "that which by nature is adjusted or proportioned to others" (Thomas Aquinas, *Summa Theologica*, II-II, Q. 57, art. 3). This point can be considered in two ways: absolutely and in itself, as in the act of procreation between man and woman, which means that in this case there is no other possibility and that this adjustment can only be thought of in terms of necessity. But it can also be considered in terms of its consequences, and we come back to the classic example of property. In itself, the possession of things is purely contingent, and a thing may belong to one individual as well as another, depending on the circumstances. Nevertheless, a critical examination of the consequences leads to the need, in the interests of social peace, for a thing to belong to a specific individual and not to just anyone, which then legitimizes the institutionalization of property in the light of the consequences.

From this it can be seen that the law of nations is natural to man according to his natural reason, which dictates it; consequently, what it prescribes does not require any specific institutionalization involving any positive act. The law of nations confirms the principle according to which man, by means of his intellect, establishes relationships and comparisons in order to deduce consequences. Thus, man's mode of being commanded by reason is indeed natural to him, since by essence his humanity is inseparable from his reason. What all nations abide by merely refracts what natural reason universally establishes in man, and is precisely identifiable with the law of nations. Nevertheless, historically, it is only as effective as its human institution.

III

From the Law of Nations to the Emergence of International Law

The source of the historical-political construction of the law of nations is to be found in the founder of international law, Francisco de Vitoria (1483-1546). The founder of the School of Salamanca substituted the term "peoples" for the term "man" in Gaius's definition, thereby making a transition from the law of individuals or private law of nations to international law between different states or public law of nations. This redefinition of the Roman concept of the law of nations creates the theoretical conditions for the establishment of a principle that regulates historical relations between nations; it assigns it a historical-political significance that moves away from its original identification with the body of natural legal law, and opens it up to a cosmopolitan requirement, the *communitas totus orbis*, understood as the universal community of peoples. As such, it incorporates the relations of citizens with other nations, as well as the duty of hospitality and the recognition of fundamental human rights for individuals and peoples.

For Vitoria, the fact that the law of nations is founded in natural law does not mean that it cannot be traced back to consent and agreement; as a result, some of its legal precepts belong to the sphere of positive law. In this sense, it is possible to invoke without contradiction a natural law of nations and a law of nations resulting from an institutional will. This gives rise to a double semantic meaning, since formally speaking, the law of nations represents one of the subdivisions of law and constitutes a standard of reference for invoking the opposition between natural law and positive law. Considered from the point of view of content, it expresses a restricted area of the legal order—that of international law—and as such encompasses the precepts of both natural law and consensual positive law. The way is thus open for the emergence of a "jusnaturalist" theory of international law. The latter implies the joint existence of a law of nations based on private consent and a law of nations based on the common consent of peoples and nations. Both are morally binding in conscience, since in their respective ways they ensure the preservation of natural law. The historical-political force of the law of nations derives from the human pact and consensus, and the human race, insofar as it constitutes a republic in its own way, asserts its power to give just laws to all. As the history of societies confirms, the community of peoples has a legislative function that regulates how States live together. Vitoria sees the law of nations as a positive law comprising a set of norms and principles that regulate international relations between peoples and nations. Such law may be either written and included in the civil law of each nation, or unwritten and introduced by consent and custom between peoples.

Thus, the idea of the sociability of all men is linked to a series of rights and duties that must be universally respected: the right to freedom of movement by land and sea, the right to free communication between nations, free trade between peoples and the right to citizenship, emigration and living in common. The elements of nature, such as air and water, forests, rivers and the sea, are common to all mankind according to natural law and the law of nations.

In line with this perspective, Vitoria initially conceives the *totus orbis* jointly as a community of moral and legal bonds. Its immanent authority is expressed in the ability to bring about a system of laws through the consent of all peoples or nations. This is initially a virtual consensus, the presence of which is attested in customary law. In this sense, in accordance with the preceding remarks, international society enjoys executive and coercive authority, because the right to the just war, as has been analyzed, is exercised by the nation suffering aggression, in accordance with the delegation of authority and the common law of the whole of humanity. If society has constituted the framework within which nature has forced man to find the means of development that will take him away from animality, the problem of the civil state and the wider problem of civilization and international society are associated in history. Civilization is the product of a set of techniques of constraint involving the deployment of artifices relating as much to political coercion as to propriety or the restrictive rules of conviviality. Constraint, which is part of the developments brought about by civilization, also takes on a political and cultural significance. The transition from *ius gentium intra se*, civil law, to *ius gentium inter se*, state law, cannot hide the fact that coercion acts as a forced legislation of appetites and reveals the use of all means to historically bring about the emergence of legality in actions. In the Vitorian problematic of history and the law of nations, the process of initially forced legislation of actions is conceptualized as a movement of perfection capable of practical evaluation and a sign of a moral humanity in the making. By the same token, civilization brings with it the possibility of equivalence between the universal legislation to which the law of nations aspires, and moralization.

This process becomes fully intelligible in Vitoria with reference to the Aristotelian theory of the four causes applied to his conception of the international community. If we invoke the efficient cause of international society, it is identifiable with the Creator of human nature and, consequently, of human sociability, which cannot be reduced to the family or national community, but which achieves its full raison d'être in relation to the universal order. The international community expresses the historical culmination of what was in germ in its condition of possibility, human nature.

Its final cause is the common good of humanity. With regard to the international community, it comprises two guiding imperatives: 1°) the preservation of international order and 2°) the growth and distribution of spiritual and material goods. The preservation of such an order presupposes the guarantee of justice and peace through respect for the independence and integrity of States and the safeguarding of the rights of the members of the international community. Just as Vitoria invoked the natural equality of all individuals, an equivalent principle must be applied to civil societies and States, which are in a position of perfect equality before natural law and the law of nations. As for the pursuit of prosperity, it must be inseparable from solidarity and mutual assistance, so that peoples are able to express the human dignity to which they are called by nature. This process is part of a logic that subordinates the particular interests of States to the common good of humanity. The law of nations thus calls on States to seek mediation towards morality that can serve as a preparation for humanity to act morally. On the one hand, for Vitoria, it is up to civilization to delimit the sphere of legality; on the other hand, it must constitute the means of reforming morals as an apprenticeship to the moral end of the rule of law. The perfection of humanity to which the law of nations aspires must make it possible to theorize the historical reality of the human race in accordance with its moral disposition. At the same time, humanity as a whole must be able to be seen as the subject of a hope for perfection. If human perfection is based on a sociable nature that men have not chosen, they must nevertheless be able to appear as the authors of their own improvement; the law of nations contributes, through the legal development of humanity that it makes possible, to understanding men as the artisans of their own perfection.

The material cause, for its part, corresponds to all its members, i.e. all the nations or states of the world; they represent the original subjects of rights and obligations in the international community. Finally, the formal cause of the community of nations is the authority that must direct it; if, whatever society we consider, authority is necessary for that society to be able to achieve its own ends, it is the same for international society. Authority must have an international scope; the whole world is precisely its original subject. Not only does Vitoria consider that authority is necessary for society to be governed and adequately oriented towards the achievement of the common good, but he also affirms the existence of a supra-state authority whose extensively envisaged purpose must lead to the common good of the earth. The result is that the general consensus of all nations is established as a legislative power 1°) through the historical and social mediation of customary law and 2°) by delegation from the universal authority, a nation is authorized to implement an executive and coercive power in the event of a just war or humanitarian intervention when populations are massacred by a tyrant.

The analogy drawn by Vitoria between the totality of the world and the political community from the point of view of their organizational structure reveals the existence of an international authority with similarities to that reigning in a republic. And this analogy can be extended when we compare the respective properties of authority in the republic and in international society: the executive, the legislature and the judiciary. This should not, however, mask the supremacy of international authority over national authority. Thus, the international community manifests a natural power constituting the root of the social structure; this power of a legislative, coercive and executive nature enables sovereigns, through a process of delegation, to apply a certain number of principles. Indeed, for example, "princes have power not only over their subjects but also over foreigners to compel them to refrain from injustice, and this by virtue of the law of nations and the authority of the whole world" (Vitoria, *Lesson on the Law of War*).

It also follows, therefore, that all the nations of the world, without distinction, remain linked together because they constitute a universal community; human societies appear to be homogeneous in all parts of the world because all men belong to the same species; there can be no difference in nature between Indians and Spaniards, which is precisely the same as affirming that, in the final analysis, we are only in a situation of cultural difference. Vitoria thus confirms the Stoic thesis of the unity of the human race, reinforced by Christianity through the affirmation of the common human dignity based on the idea that all men are created in the image of God. Nevertheless, there is a distinction between being and acting: man is in the image of the Creator through his being, regardless of the use he may or may not make of his potential or the way in which he uses it. The use of reason is in fact a principle that equalizes all men; by gaining access to it (as Vitoria points out, children have rights even though they are not in a position to exercise them on their own), every man, even if he does not know God, is in a position to act morally. It is with reference to the possession of free will that the condition of knowledge of good and evil appears, as well as the possibility of wishing them and fulfilling them. Everyone is in a position to know what he ought to do by the natural light of reason. Man is indeed a moral being, and his morality derives from his rational nature.

The law of nations thus extends equality in dignity to all nations that have common rights and obligations; it is recognition of this homogeneity and of the powers that flow from our natural sociability. This is demonstrated precisely by the fact that natural law ignores differences between people. The universal common good embraces national rights and is accompanied by obligations of justice and solidarity that serve to make it effective. In this sense, humanity constitutes a homogeneous community, and this community does not depend solely on the arbitrary will of man; it is immanent in the natural order and thereby acquires normative power.

If nature only seems to be confronted with relations of force that give rise to other relations of force, the problem for the law of nations is to introduce the language of value into a cultural history that will enable us to assess progress towards the better. Nations must impose reciprocal constraints on each other so that the freedom of one limits that of the other until a global freedom is achieved. The initial uprooting of man from nature analyzed in the *Lesson on Political Power* must be understood as equivalent to the conquest of his true destination, the path of which is mapped out by the law of nations. And this destination is not a purely indeterminate one; it leads him to strive to become a good man. *Communitas totus orbis* effectively reveals humanity as a being with a destination. It is up to civilization to confirm humanity's destination of transnatural perfection by revealing, through historical mutations, the signs of such a transhistorical destiny.

In this sense, civilization is a moment equivalent to a conversion of human destiny, henceforth articulated, as civil and international society show, by the means of law. It is precisely the task of the law of nations to endorse the observation that it is humanity as a whole, and not just political society, that provides the basis for continuous improvement. In addition to the natural development of human capacities requiring the mediation of reason, there is the cultural and legal development of a collective humanity. Nature having bestowed reason and virtue on man, and having rescued him "from the shipwreck", it is clear that at the source of the cultural and juridical history of humanity are dispositions and potentialities; without these, man would be condemned to the precariousness and unhappiness of his condition. The final development of such historicity is expressed in law, civil society and international society, which structure the progress of civilization. The reformation of humanity's way of being together in history therefore reveals an original agreement with nature and a departure from nature. The experience of the discovery of the New World simply confirms that man is malleable and perfectible, and that all ignorance can therefore be overcome. This is the social function of language, as an instrument for transmitting ideas and a prerequisite for knowledge, the very raison d'être of which is to be communicable. It is the link by which people relate to one another, and everything cultural ultimately comes down to language. If knowledge could be assumed to exist independently of language, it would ultimately be confronted with its own incommunicability and poverty.

The transmission of knowledge within the social group enables the individual to enter into a continuous process of self-improvement, thus fulfilling his ontological purpose of actualizing the potentialities immanent in his being. Without sociability, language would be non-existent, and man would have no sense of justice or friendship; there is no denying that the relationship with others, under certain conditions, contributes to our perfection and plays an indispensable role in our access to happiness. This link to others is an essential condition for autonomy. It is both a necessity and a good, because it cannot be reduced to the simple satisfaction of material desires. It is the condition for moving from the ontological status of the individual to the ethical status of the person. Education, particularly through the necessary mediator of understanding, is the primary cause of the structuring of future moral existence. Indeed, through education and instruction, individual access to the use of reason becomes possible. The educational value of communication contributes to the possibility of inter-generational sharing, also in terms of modes of action, by taking as its guiding principle the natural light of reason, the use of which initially requires the mediation of others in order to avoid the ever-present possibility of error, man being what he is through his relationship with others. Historically, education confirms the need to conform to a collective discipline, thus revealing moralization as man's destination.

It is also clear from these observations that civilization expresses a moment corresponding to a conversion of human destiny which, as the Vitorian concept of *totus orbis* shows, is inseparable from the means of law and, broadly considered, from the law of nations. The aforementioned homogeneity of the human race establishes that it is collective humanity and not the isolated individual that forms the basis of continuous improvement. There is a supplement to the natural development of the physical race from the initial destitution of the individual: the cultural development of a civilized species. Education and civilization make the development of human potential the driving principle of cultural history. Recognition of natural human weakness and the physical ills that flow from it, inseparable from the distress of an existence in struggle, leads us to recognize that, at the root of its development and the growth of its primary skills, we could invoke, in the manner of the Epicureans, a necessary causality. The means that nature uses, namely reason, freedom and virtue, have the function of legitimizing the fact that they are not identifiable with the production resulting from the multiple encounters of atoms combining in an infinite and purposeless manner, ultimately equivalent to a blind necessity involving a combination of actions and reactions of natural physical forces. Vitoria appeals to a providential purpose in order to make intelligible the increase in human forces and dispositions as an unconditional affirmation of the value of life. In terms of the history of nature and the resulting history of societies, confrontation is a constant in empirical history. How, then, can we escape the inevitability of a blind necessity that we find again at the international level, at the very moment when we have tried to free ourselves from it in order to make the initial development of humanity intelligible? How can we escape the affirmation of the absurdity of human history? This is the function of the law of nations: to find an appropriate way of exercising reason.

As the *Lesson on the Law of War* showed, if conflict cannot be abolished, a way is open to create the conditions for its management, or even its overcoming. The genesis of political society had shown how the clash of concupiscences was overcome by the equal subjection of individuals to the common constraint of political power. In this sense, this clash can be saved from the impasse of absolute nonsense, because it carries within it the cause of its own overcoming. The conflict of concupiscences can only lead—from the point of view of a providential finality invoked by Vitoria—to the imperative of the reciprocal perfection of individuals. By favoring the means that nature uses, providential finality offers a model for interpreting the political contribution of constraint, by demonstrating a conception of the ordered composition of concupiscences that ensures protection and preservation. Two principles of social structuring thus enter into competition, that of concupiscence restrained by mutual friction and that of the homogenization of the social body achieved by the coercion of political power.

As for the law of nations, it responds to the homogenization of the human race in the following way: historically, it has taken on a range of forms as many acceptances of cultural diversity, emanating directly from natural law or recognized through custom by all peoples and nations. Thus, for Vitoria, the right to free communication and free movement of people throughout the different parts of the world is identifiable as a fundamental right intended to legitimize the entry of the Spanish into the territories of the New World. It was a manifest expression of the law of nations, tacitly accepted by the unanimous consent of all nations, which can be illustrated, for example, by the sacred duty of hospitality towards foreigners. Humanity must be governed by ethical and social principles such as hospitality, which form part of our way of being together; this observation has its origins in the community of goods that originally characterized the natural condition of human beings. The distribution of land and the establishment of political boundaries have disrupted the perpetuation of this customary heritage. In the light of history, however, it is clear that the formation of these different nationalities cannot conceal a common defense of the right of free communication, which for Vitoria is nothing more than a manifestation of the friendship and harmony that should ensure union between people.

Thus, in a more complex way than the family, all society constitutes an organic whole of reciprocal utility. With friendship, Vitoria looks beyond the objective social relationships that separate as much as they unite, to find a closer bond, which can only be founded in the feeling of a profound similarity between people. Because nature and society make individuals dissimilar, they can wish to be similar, and friendship expresses an essential identity behind a persistent difference. In this sense, social and moral life implies closeness between man as man and man, in other words, as fellow human beings; it organizes links that bring about the necessary differences in a just complementarily. Nature seems to be the synthesis of these two necessities. On the one hand, it is the source of the similarity between human beings and the reason for the pleasure derived from their association. On the other hand, it is identifiable with what lies at the foundation of the hierarchical relationships of the family, giving them a kind of extension into the city.

From the point of view of humankind, the law of nations reinforces the fact that what nations and individuals provide for each other is not generally identical, since no one needs what he already has. Nevertheless, an examination of the law of nations should not obscure the difference it implies between what is just and what is useful; the former cannot be dissociated from a specific imperative of value; as a prerequisite to any exchange, there must be a distribution of benefits proportional to the commitments of each party, in a manner analogous to what happens in civil society. The just must have regard to both civil society and the international community; it is up to the just to establish what is appropriate for each person, and then to ensure that a distribution is maintained through exchanges. As for the search for what is useful, this derives from the respective appreciation of the parties; now it is clear that the parties do not aim at exchange if the inequality between them is too great; once exchange has been instituted, these same parties do not have to appreciate the share due to each, but only the equality of what each gives and receives. From the intra-state and inter-state points of view, justice and utility express an imperative of equalization while accommodating inequality, the former establishing and maintaining well-founded inequalities, the latter disregarding them as far as possible, but attributing content to themselves on the basis of differences constituting the principle of complete complementarily. In accordance with these two spheres of inter-human relations, the purpose of justice is to regulate the existence of any community, as required by the inadequacy of human beings in relation to themselves; the law of nations merely confirms this by invoking the notions of equality and reciprocity that constitute friendship between peoples. In this sense, international politics must respond to the imperative of the evangelical law of love of neighbor (the transition from self-love to charity being founded on the identity of rational nature between human beings), thus rediscovering the Aristotelian perspective of politics understanding *philia* as having as its end the common life, society having as its end the good life. In civil society, recourse to others makes it possible to think in terms of self-sufficiency, and in the law of nations, in order to ensure the continuity of this perspective it makes it possible to give effect to a project to unify the nature of man and relations between men. It is therefore clear to Vitoria that the international community, as the union of the whole earth, expresses a unity based on the principles of human sociability and communication.

Freedom of the seas and freedom of navigation also represent a right that cannot be dissociated from the right to free communication; it merely confirms for another specific area the "*ius peregrinandi*" that can be extended from land to sea. Vitoria refers to the origin of such an identifiable right to the right of discovery as exemplified by the voyage of Christopher Columbus. Thus, in accordance with the law of nations and natural law, what is left abandoned becomes the property of the person who seizes it. At the same time, Vitoria confirms the legacy of Roman law invoking the community of seas, rivers and ports, and measures the scope of this change in this specific case from a right to *ius commune*. In Roman law, the sea was characterized as a *res communis*, as were the air, the water of rivers and shorelines. The common use of these goods is based on natural law, which means that anyone can benefit from them, build on the shore or establish a fishery without claiming ownership. From this perspective, the sea is defined as *res nullius* in terms of the wealth it offers. There is, however, a restriction: in the case of navigation, there is no compatibility between common use and the claim to a monopoly of an occupation; such a right only makes sense in relation to the freedom it implies. The Roman people are defined as judges (*arbitror* qualifying the power of the Roman people by *juridictio*) over the maritime shores without claiming to exercise domination in the form of *imperium*. As far as the public dimension of these areas is concerned, only public power has the power to emancipate from the prerogatives of *usus omnium*.

Vitoria conceives of this right over the seas as a public right that is not reducible to the individual sphere but also concerns States; the result is that it is impossible for any nation whatsoever to exercise any jurisdiction over the seas. The extensive understanding resulting from the conception of such a right naturally has the consequence of positioning the principle of freedom of the seas in the name of the community of goods; but by accepting such a legal vacuum, it is surreptitiously reintroducing force as a measure of the right of discovery. Nevertheless, freedom of the seas must respond to the inalienable principle of free movement, which is indissociable from the right to navigate freely throughout the oceans and to have the effective means to do so. It is therefore necessary for all nations to be able to use ports and shores so that their ships can drop anchor and have the necessary time to be ready to set sail again. Ultimately, Vitoria wants to put an end to the monopoly power of certain states over maritime space.

On the basis of these remarks, one point remains to be clarified. To clarify it, we need to go back to Aristotle and refer to Suarez's explanations on this question. This concerns the division made by jurists within the law of nations into primary and secondary law; to do this, it is necessary to refer to the common definition invoked by Aristotle between the natural order as that which possesses the same power in any place and the legal order as that which is established by convention and particularizes natural justice. In fact, the distinction between natural political justice and legal justice does not imply opposition, given that the former, by virtue of its generality (it is proper to any political community to punish crime) requires in its historical incarnation to be particularized in the form of positive laws, simply expressing by this that, for legal political justice, the law is subject to variations. There is no opposition between the former and the latter, since the positive order implies the indispensable fulfillment of the natural. If physical nature is indeed immutable, the same cannot be said of human nature, which is characterized by its plasticity. It follows that variability is not a criterion of unnaturalness, any more than uniformity would be a criterion of adequacy to nature.

IV

Necessity of the Distinction between the Law of Nations and Natural Law in Sixteenth-Century Second Scholasticism

The non-contradictory link between natural law and the law of nations derives its condition of possibility from the Aristotelian thesis according to which there is no obstacle to positing natural law as variable without this mutability divesting it of its specificity as natural law, while making intelligible the fact that natural law is not always and identically the same. Authentic natural law is that which adjusts to an essentially mutable human nature, which amounts to deducing that the mutability of laws is not a sign of their artificiality, but that the abstract universality requiring the identity of laws in all places is ultimately unnatural. Just as, for Aristotle, it is legitimate to recognize, without contradiction, in reference to natural law, that differences (historical and geographical) between peoples imply differences between laws, so we can recognize, without contradiction, in reference to natural law, that the history of nations and their evolution imply differences in the law of nations (as the example of slavery has shown). For Aristotle, it also appears that such a recognition can only lead to the assertion that natural law is singularized in order to be adequate to the diversity of nature. The mutability of natural law and positive law is to be considered in two different ways, since the variations of the former are necessary from the point of view of form and content, whereas the variations of the latter are necessary only in their form, which implies that the content is contingent and cannot be deduced from any principle, even if it is necessary for variable positive law to exist, as well as conventions and customs.

In line with this heritage, Suarez, in accordance with his desire to refund the law of nations, maintains the division between natural and positive law. It should be noted in this respect that the laws of the law of nations are not purely natural and, according to the division invoked, can only be positive and human. The fact that it is rooted in custom confirms its mutability, and this is precisely where it differs from natural law. For, as historical development shows, there was no need for the preservation and progress of the human race for mankind to form a single political community. The Roman Empire itself never exercised total sovereignty over the peoples over whom it had power. The Law of Nations confirms historically that there has never been a sovereign political body in humanity. The fact that there has been no sovereign body politic does not rule out the constitution of a relative universality (as distinct from the absolute universality of natural law) corresponding to a communal unity in the making, seeking to establish reciprocal obligations.

At the end of these remarks, in order not to perpetuate the confusions fostered by tradition, it is indeed advisable to avoid in the suarezian perspective a reduction of the law of nations to natural law. According to the contribution of Thomas Aquinas, it appears that natural law and the law of nations represent rights that are indissociable from what makes man human. The former concerns man from the point of view of his animality—i.e. his generic nature—but also from the point of view of his belonging to the whole, and orders in him tendencies that go beyond the species to which he belongs. The second refers to man's specific difference, such as his specifically historical and political nature. In Suarez's view, a careful examination of natural law leads us to refuse to accept that it is common to men and animals, and consequently to attribute to it a sensitive nature as its foundation. For if natural law is indeed in conformity with the conservation of sensitive nature, this remains in the mode of rationality. The affirmative precepts internal to natural law base their obligatory nature on rational evidence according to a necessary deduction from first principles, those of human nature.

It nevertheless appears that 1°) the principles of the law of nations, despite their specific universality, do not cover such an intrinsic necessity. 2°) The law of nations does not have an intrinsically moral value and it is not possible for it to take as its reference conclusions necessarily inferred from moral principles. The precepts implied by the latter are constitutive of natural law. Indeed, it can be said that what is derived from natural principles by means of reasoning that is self-evident is ultimately inscribed in the human heart. The universality of natural law is immanent in human nature, while at the same time implying reference to a transcendent origin. It is therefore absolute. By contrast, the origin of the law of nations is not immediately linked to a theory of human being, since its dominant feature lies in the fact that men have historically instituted its precepts in almost the entire human community. This universality, when we take into account the socio-historical development of peoples, is relative because it is not based on a reading of human nature, but on the free will and consent of men. These last two elements, which are specific to its conventional dimension, are likely to be valid for the whole of humanity, without necessarily having an identical justification or foundation. While the content of the precept of natural law corresponds to what is good or bad in itself, that of the law of nations concerns what is evaluated as such on the basis of common consent. We conclude that 1°) the universality of natural law is absolute because it is defined by its uniqueness and immutability; it transcends political and historical reality as a constitutive fact of man's humanity. 2°) The universality of the law of nations is relative because of a) the artificial nature of its existence, and b) its origin in the consensus of the greatest number at a given historical moment.

The "quasi-political and moral unity" inherent in the law of nations is indeed a unity that is necessarily relative to the historical development of humanity, since it remains partly dependent on the sovereignty of each State. Nevertheless, the law of nations historically supports the ontological principle of human sociability and the anthropological principle of interhumanity. Its theorization is based on the concept of *universitas* bequeathed by the Middle Ages, a sign of an ontology of totality, of *totus orbis* comprising humanity as a synthesis of all the peoples constituted as States. The transition from the multitude of peoples in the historical future to an organized association within the limits of respect for the sovereignty of States remains possible and desirable. In this way, the effectiveness of a human universal based on the recognition of a common nature between all individuals that constitutes them as human beings is historically consolidated. The suarezian understanding of the law of nations brings out in historical practice the effects of this understanding of the being of the human, at the crossroads of the heritage of Stoic anthropology and Christian thought which structures a universal community of the human race expressing a specific entity: that of a being-in-common. It aims to promote a representation of humanity that becomes legitimate only when it is theorized in the universal. This is the culmination of the process of replacing the *cosmos* of Antiquity with *universitas*, in order to advance from the reference to the divine order to a dimension of politics that is specific to the totality and a globalizing conception of the human being. With the law of nations, we see the emergence of the fact that humanity is no longer a part of the totality; it is now in the process of being identified with a totality in the making, which is its own law.

On the one hand, the law of nations confirms the relative dimension of the legitimacy of state power, and on the other, it frees the state from its historical isolation by introducing it into a community of law based on the unity of the human race. Its function is precisely intelligible from the point of view of an international political order, and in this respect it differs from civil law. The function of civil law, which is an act of the human will, is to integrate human beings into a body politic for the purpose of mutual assistance. However, this unity per se is not historically achieved; it requires the mediation of the law of nations. The theoretical framework is thus laid out, reminding us that human nature has historically been embodied in a multiplicity of states, and that its intelligibility is inseparable from its embodiment in historical development. In accordance with the preceding anthropo-theological deductions, it then becomes necessary to invoke a right which, by virtue of its relative universality, stands apart from all other rights. It is thus the expression of freedom and reason in history, and not the product of a logical deduction from human nature, but it is nonetheless historically beneficial to the affirmation of that same nature.

The specific original function of the law of nations is mutual assistance between nations, the preservation of peace and justice in inter-human relations through the mediation of common consent and common laws. Its emergence is not historically explicable on the basis of positive decrees, but on the basis of a set of legal norms introduced in time through custom and the ongoing practice of nations as effective members of the community of nations as a universalization in the making. The law of nations is therefore a stakeholder in the objective externalization of human nature over time. From this perspective, it confirms that humanity merges with its history, just as the existence of the individual merges with its duration. And it makes it necessary to question the status of freedom in the temporality with which the theory of the State will be confronted, given that the historical situation of peoples also determines the possibilities of political action.

This relationship with history makes it possible to refine the difference between natural law and the law of nations. The object of the former is not humanity understood historically as a unit divided into States, but humanity understood ontologically as a unit composed of all men; every man considered individually is nevertheless in himself a manifestation of his natural right. If we refer to the object of the law of nations, it can be assimilated to nations as members of humanity, its function being to regulate inter-state relations in the course of history; it thus asserts itself in its public dimension by seeking to guarantee peace and justice in the inter-community space.

Historically, it appears that the precepts of the law of nations are more general than those of civil law, precisely because "the interests of humanity as a whole and conformity with the first and universal principles of nature" (Suarez, *Of the Laws*, II, 20, n. 2) are taken into account. Nevertheless, the need for such conformity cannot ignore the mutability of the law of nations, since it depends on human consent. Its prohibitions and positive precepts are thereby affected, since it has been established that its rules cannot be derived from natural principles by means of necessary and obvious deductions and that the basis of its obligation does not derive from pure reason but implies reference to a human obligation based on custom. This historical mutability only requires effective authority as a condition of possibility. The historical understanding underlying this thesis, by recognizing the unity of the individual and the social environment, affirms the particularity of nations and the relativity of wills; a synthesis is thus achieved of the person and humanity with the unfolding of their temporal existence. With the law of nations, man appears to himself as a historical being and as a social being, asserting his particularity while trying to account for it in thought. He discovers that he is part of a collectivity participating in a common history that is also common to several collectivities. At the same time, he confirms that it is possible for human beings to define and situate themselves in relation to their fellow human beings as they become historically different.

It is then possible, in relation to this observation, to distinguish a double historical manifestation of the law of nations: one (international law) whose universal character results from the recognition of a common law by several nations, and the other (customary law) which is truly universal because of its conformity to the universality of habits and customs; this advent is therefore purely human.

V

Historical Justification of the Law of Nations

It was up to the School of natural law, with Grotius (1583-1645) as its founder, and its emblematic representatives, Samuel Pufendorf (1632-1694), Jean Barbeyrac (1674-1744) and Jean-Jacques Burlamaqui (1694-1748), to continue establishing the theoretical foundations of the central concepts of political thought, of which the law of nations, such as inalienable rights, the social contract and sovereignty, form part. Such law, by virtue of being consistent with the principles of reason and human dignity, is at the service of peace; it is voluntary and positive, historically established through the mediation of consensus by peoples constituted as sovereign states. Its binding force results from the will of all the peoples or, at the very least, of a majority of them.

In Burlamaqui's view, an examination of the historical constitution of states should make it possible to envisage a form of society, one specific to the general system of humanity that is analogous to the one existing naturally between men. From this perspective, the function of the law of nations is to determine the conditions under which different peoples will be able to coexist in harmony. With the Law of Nations, Burlamaqui's legal thinking extended the concept of citizenship by attributing to it the right of the human race. Whether we consider people or states, they are historically led to understand themselves as elements of a universal human society. This society goes beyond national citizenship and brings the human race together in the unity of its purpose, the two predominant features of which are peace and justice.

From this point of view, Burlamaqui believes that the law of nations has a cosmopolitan purpose, which could legitimately be compared to the law of nations invoked by Stoicism, in particular Cicero's theses on the universal society of humankind. Cicero associates a cosmological and cosmopolitan orientation with it; in fact, the law that results from it is cosmic and natural because its rule is the identity of nature between men considered as reasonable beings. Nevertheless, for Burlamaqui, this cosmopolitan vision refers to a communitarian horizon, openness towards the future and the possible, reflecting a refusal to reduce man's humanity to its historical positivity. If we consider the rights of a people in relation to the destination of the human species, they appear to be effectively cosmopolitan, and their fulfillment presupposes the limitation and overcoming of national sovereignties in an association that conforms to the natural law of nations. Consequently, it is the duty of nations to attribute to each other the right to exist where they are established, and thereby to recognize each other as full citizens of a common world of humankind. This cosmopolitan right is therefore inseparable from the quest for peaceful coexistence.

Thus, for Burlamaqui, it is necessary to rectify the thesis of the law of nations defended by Grotius, which endeavors to assign a legal dimension to war; such a thesis should instead seek a legal state that guarantees the imperatives of collective happiness and peaceful coexistence. We need to turn the problem on its head: instead of limiting ourselves to establishing a jurisdiction in the state of nature between peoples, we need to determine, by means of natural law (whose principles are as follows: the duty to recognize the universal equality of men, the duty not to harm others and to repair the damage inflicted, the duty of mutual benevolence and the duty to keep one's commitments), the legal state that can put an end to the predominance of power relations between nations.

The various historical and political manifestations of the law of nations result from the application of the rational aptitudes by which man accomplishes the ends of the natural law that the Creator has deployed in this world. For Burlamaqui, therefore, there is a respective contribution by God the lawgiver and the power of human rationality to establish laws, both in the intra-state sphere and in the inter-state sphere, of the law of nations. The latter historically confirms the anthropological principle of human sociability and the theological foundation of natural law. It also expresses in historical action the effects of an understanding of the human being (i.e. the affirmation of a common nature between all individuals that constitutes them precisely as human beings) derived from the heritage of the Stoic conception of man and Christian thought, and inseparable from a universal community of humankind.

A solution to the problem of the nature of the link to be established between natural law and the law of nations is entirely possible for Burlamaqui. It consists in distinguishing between two types of law of nations. In order to do this, it is necessary to take advantage of Pufendorf's legacy concerning his definition and understanding of alliances and pacts in the constitution of relations between men and in the conduct of the political life of States. Not only is political law destined, by virtue of its foundation in the nature of man, to expand historically into a cosmopolitan law, but it must be distinguished from the conception bequeathed by Roman law, according to which it would be identifiable with the totality of rules established by natural reason between all men and which would be equally binding on all peoples. At the same time as the distinction between natural law and the law of nations is being drawn, the founding function of the former in relation to all legal normativity cannot be overlooked. In return, the alliances and pacts concluded between nations proceed to a precise extension of the commitments specific to the duties of natural law. On the one hand, the law of nations must not contradict the maxims of natural law, such as "not to harm one another" (Pufendorf, *Le droit de la nature et des gens*, I, VIII, IX, § II); on the other hand, by respecting this initial condition, the law of nations participates in a precise historical and political delimitation of the possibility of its application, so that the consensus of the greatest number of nations is achieved.

As a result, there are alliances "by which one commits oneself to something more than what was otherwise due by virtue of the natural law common to all men" (*Ibid.*, VIII, IX, § III). In Pufendorf's view, this confirms that the necessary adherence to the maxims of natural law understood as the foundations and regulating principles of the law of nations, does not exclude recognition of the value and organizing function of political law in establishing and preserving understanding between nations. There is therefore an absolute necessity for positive law in the historical construction of the inter-state bond.

Ch. 5: Historical Justification of the Law of Nations 65

Burlamaqui's distinction between the two forms of law of nations from the point of view of their origin and nature confirms Pufendorf's theses. When the law of nations is universal and has an obligatory value in itself, such as the pursuit of peace by all just means, it is in no real way different from natural law, its immutability being a sign of the unconditional nature of the duties towards humanity, which cannot suffer any dispensation, whether on the part of sovereigns or private individuals. It is such that even an agreement between all nations could not claim to abrogate it; Burlamaqui finds in this definition the Ciceronian accents characterizing "the true law" identical to right reason, "spread throughout all beings, always in agreement with itself", "one and the same eternal and immutable law, which governs all nations and at all times" (Cicero, *On the Republic*, III, § XXII). From this perspective, there is an ontological identity between the law of nations and natural law, because they overlap in principle and purpose to such an extent that they can only be distinguished nominally, since they both refer to an unconditional and transhistorical obligation that formally prohibits any derogation. And, as Pufendorf pointed out, strict observance of natural law would enable humankind to render reference to customs, which are based on the mere agreement of peoples, superfluous.

The second form of the law of nations, on the other hand, confirms its distinction from natural law because it is based on a conventional act involving the creative force of reason and freedom. As a result, it cannot claim to be universal, since it is binding only on those who have voluntarily agreed to abide by it; which is to say that recognition of the arbitrary nature of its origin also implies recognition of the arbitrary nature of its modification or abrogation. Furthermore, as Barbeyrac points out, what means do we have, when we refer to relations between peoples, to determine what degree of repetition of acts and what length of time are necessary for a custom to acquire binding force? From this division made by Burlamaqui, we can understand the origin of the relativist and skeptical theses concerning the possibility of the immutability of the law of nations. Their consequence is the definitive separation between morality and politics. But if it is true that politics cannot be confused with morality, we can assume that Burlamaqui would unreservedly agree with what Rousseau wrote: "Those who wish to treat politics and morality separately will never understand either of them" (*Emile*, Book IV).

Conclusion

It was on the basis of the complex heritage analyzed above that Grotius, who played an emblematic role in the history of the development of public international law, drew a distinction between positive international law and natural law. According to the founder of the School of Natural Law, the law of nations is a constituent part of human law and the force of the obligation it generates results from the "consent of all States, or at least of the greatest number" (Grotius, *On the Law of War and Peace, Preliminary Discourse*, § XVIII). In this way, the law of nations has been able to set out the rules of law with which States are obliged to comply, for example before the outbreak of hostilities (*ius ad bellum*, right to war), during the outbreak of hostilities (*ius in bello*, during war) and at the time of peace treaties (law after war). The doctrine of the law of nations is inseparable from the definition of war as "the state of those who attempt to settle their differences by force" (*Ibid.*, Volume I, Book I, Ch. II, § 2). The function of war, in the absence of agreement on justice between nations, is both to bring about peace and to replace international justice. The effectiveness of the law of nations lies in its ability to offer an alternative to the absence of justice by implementing justice through the use of force. In this sense, one of the sometimes contested functions of the law of nations is to spell out the conditions for waging a just war.

It seems fair to say that the diversity of these issues will find in the French Declaration of Human Rights of 1789 a possible historical reconciliation of natural law and the law of nations, by confirming precisely the role of the latter in shaping the legal future of humanity.

Jean-Paul Coujou

Bibliography

Aristote, *Ethique à Nicomaque*, Paris, Vrin, 1959, traduction par J. Tricot.

Cicéron, *Traité des devoirs* in *Les Stoïciens*, Paris, Gallimard, 1962, traduction par E. Bréhier.

Gaius, *Institutes*, Paris, Les Belles Lettres, 1950, texte établi et traduit par J. Reinach.

Grotius, *Du droit de la guerre et de la paix*, réimpression, Caen, Bibliothèque de philosophie politique de l'Université de Caen, 1984, 2 volumes.

Isidore de Séville, *Etymologiae*, Patrologia Latina, Migne, 82, 73-728.

Suárez, *Opera Omnia*, éditions Vivès, Paris, 1856-1877, volume 5, *De legibus (I-V)*.

- *Des lois et du Dieu législateur. Livres I-II*, Paris, Dalloz, 2003, introduction et traduction par J.-P. Coujou.

Thomas d'Aquin, *Somme théologique*, édition coordonnée par A. Raulin, traduction par A. M. Roguet, 4 volumes, Paris, Cerf, 1984-1986.

Vitoria, *Comentarios del Maestro Francisco de Vitoria a la Secunda Secundae de Santo Tomás*, édition de V. Beltrán de Heredia, 6 vol., Biblioteca de Teólogos Españoles, Salamanque, 1932-1952.

- *Leçons sur les Indiens et sur le droit de guerre*, Genève, Librairie Droz, 1966, traduction par M. Barbier.

- *Leçon sur le pouvoir civil*, Paris, Vrin, 1980, Traduction par M. Barbier.

- T. Urdanoz, *Obras de Francisco de Vitoria: Relecciones teológicas*, edición crítica del texto latino, versión española, introducción general e introducciones con el estudio de su doctrina teológico-jurídica, Madrid, Biblioteca de Autores Cristianos, 1960.

Other works by the author

30. En préparation: *L'émergence du devenir juridique de l'humanité. Vitoria.*
29. *Ethique et politique dans la philosophie du Siècle d'Or espagnol*, à paraître, 500 p.
28. *Nature humaine et pouvoir politique chez Gracian*, à paraître.

27. *Pacte social et souveraineté politique chez Burlamaqui,* Paris, Garnier, 2024, 250 p.
26. *Ensayos sobre la filosofía del siglo de Oro,* Madrid, Sindéresis, 2024, 300 p.
25. *Suárez dans l'histoire de la métaphysique. II, La postérité,* à paraître, Entremise Editions Paris, 720 p., 2023.
24. *Philosophies du Siècle d'Or espagnol. Figures de la pensée juridique et politique,* Honoré Champion, Paris, 2022, 500 p.
23. *Suárez dans l'histoire de la métaphysique. I. L'héritage. Le débat contemporain,* sous presse, Entremise Editions Paris, 238 p., 2022.
22. *Innerarity. Ethique pour une humanité postmoderne,* préface de Daniel Innerarity, Uppreditions, Paris, 2017, 420 p.
21. *Aux origines du droit international. Le droit des gens,* Uppreditions, Paris, 2015, (2ème édition 2016) 80 p.
20. *Vitoria. Le fondement éthique de la justice,* Etude et traduction, Dalloz, 2014, 427 p.
19. *Bibliografía vitoriana,* en collaboration avec M. Idoya Zorroza, Pampelune, Cuadernos de Pensamiento Español, 2014, 167 p.

18. *Droit, anthropologie et politique chez Suárez*, Artège, Perpignan, 2012, 616 p. En cours de traduction en espagnol.
17. *Pensée de l'être et théorie politique. Le moment suarézien. III*, 350 p., Louvain, Peeters, 2012, Prix Charles Lévêque de l'Institut de France, Académie des Sciences morales et politiques.
16. *Pensée de l'être et théorie politique. Le moment suarézien. II*, 247 p., Louvain, Peeters, 2012, Prix Charles Lévêque.
15. *Pensée de l'être et théorie politique. Le moment suarézien. I*, 300 p., Louvain, Peeters, 2011, Prix Charles Lévêque.
14. *Bibliografía suareciana*, Cuadernos de Pensamiento Español, Pampelune, 2010, Université de Navarre, 170 p.
13. *Suárez. Quelle communauté d'être pour le Créateur et la créature ? La légitimité de la théologie à l'épreuve de la question de l'analogie de l'étant. Disputes métaphysiques XXVIII-XXIX*, (Thomas d'Aquin, Cajetan, Diego Mas, Suárez), 300 p., Grenoble, Jérôme Millon, 2009.
12. *Vitoria. La question de l'homicide à la lumière du droit divin et du droit naturel. A la recherche de*

l'effectivité de l'exigence théologico-éthique. Leçon sur l'homicide, traduction annotée, (90 p.) 2009, Paris, Dalloz.

11. *Droit naturel et humanité chez Burlamaqui* (300 p.), avec une édition critique de l'ouvrage de Burlamaqui : *Principes du droit naturel*, 200 p., Paris, Dalloz, 2007, 500 p.

10. *Philosophie politique et ontologie. II.* (Rousseau-Kant), Paris, L'Harmattan, 2006, 207 p.

9. *Philosophie politique et ontologie. I.* (Platon, Aristote, Suárez, Hobbes, Spinoza), 370 p., Paris, L'Harmattan, 2006, préface de M. B. Bourgeois de l'Académie des Sciences Morales et Politiques.

8. Participation à l'édition digitalisée intégrale en 2004 des « *Disputes métaphysiques* » de Suárez en latin sur Internet (*D.M.* 44 et 54) sous la direction du Pr. S. Castellote Cubells à Valence (Espagne) et en collaboration avec le Pr. J.-P. Doyle (U.S.A.), et le Pr. M. Renemann (Bochum), internet: scc@salvadorcastellote.com, 250 p.

7. *La politique ontologique de Suárez. Des lois et du Dieu législateur (Livres I-II)*, Introduction : « La

politique ontologique de Suárez » (81 p.), Paris, Dalloz, 2003, 688 p. (2° édition, mars 2005).

6. *Suárez. Les êtres de raison et l'extension logique du champ de l'ontologie. Dispute LIV*, Introduction : « L'extension logique du champ de l'ontologie », Paris, Vrin, 2001, 204 p.

5. *Le vocabulaire de Suárez*, Paris, Ellipses, 2001, 60 p.

4. *Suárez. La généalogie d'une ontologie de l'essence. La distinction de l'étant fini et de son être. Dispute métaphysique XXXI*, Introduction : « La généalogie d'une ontologie de l'essence », Paris, Vrin, 1999, 289 p.

3. *Suárez et la refondation de la métaphysique comme ontologie*, (avec la traduction de l' « Index détaillé de la Métaphysique d'Aristote ») Peeters, (Philosophes médiévaux, T. 38) Louvain, 1999, 309 p. (67*p., 242 p.).

2. *Suárez et la renaissance de la métaphysique. Disputes métaphysiques I-III*, Introduction : « Suárez et la renaissance de la métaphysique », Paris, Vrin, 1998, 344 p.

1. *Politiques de l'ontologie et horizon communautaire*, Atelier national de reproduction des

thèses, Lille, 1994, 2 volumes, 1° volume : pp. 1-426 ; 2° volume : pp. 427-835.

B. Direction d'ouvrages

L'Etat et le pouvoir, Domuni Press, Bruxelles, octobre 2016, 242 p.

Problématiques du contrat social, PU de l'ICT, 2018, 240 p.

C. Ouvrage collectif

- *Brill Companion to Suárez*, USA/ Netherlands, Brills, 2014, 383 p. Contribution sur la philosophie politique de Suárez (*Suarez's Legal and Political Thought*) pp. 29–71.
- *Brill Companion on Leibniz's Thought and Activities*, 2024, *Political rationality, international balance and the duty of historical hope in Suárez (1548–1617) and Leibniz (1646–1716)* (*Rationalité politique, équilibre international et devoir d'espérance historique chez Suárez (1548–1617) et Leibniz (1646–1716)*).

About the Author

Jean-Paul Coujou, member of the Institut Michel Villey, Agrégé de philosophie chaire supérieure, doctor (Paris I) HDR (Paris IV), honorary professor at the Faculty of Philosophy of the Institut catholique de Toulouse, where he was director of the Ethics, Philosophy, Science and Society laboratory as well as director of the doctoral cycle, is the author of some thirty books, around a hundred articles and winner of the Prix Charles Lévêque from the Académie des Sciences morales et politiques in 2012. He has also been a visiting professor at a number of foreign universities.

www.ingramcontent.com/pod-product-compliance
Lightning Source LLC
Chambersburg PA
CBHW060849050426
42453CB00008B/911